CW00657754

Dave lives and works in Southampton. By day he is an accountant, by night a dreamer and a doer, a writer and presenter, a person with an unbridled passion for sharing happiness and joy. He believes life is for living, every day is a good day and we all get to choose.

Dave Redman

THINK AMAZING
BE AMAZING

'A Life Philosophy'

AUSTIN MACAULEY PUBLISHERS™

LONDON • CAMBRIDGE • NEW YORK • SHARJAH

Copyright © Dave Redman (2017)

The right of Dave Redman to be identified as author of this work has been asserted by him in accordance with section 77 and 78 of the Copyright, Designs and Patents Act 1988.

All rights reserved. No part of this publication may be reproduced, stored in a retrieval system, or transmitted in any form or by any means, electronic, mechanical, photocopying, recording, or otherwise, without the prior permission of the publishers.

Any person who commits any unauthorized act in relation to this publication may be liable to criminal prosecution and civil claims for damages.

A CIP catalogue record for this title is available from the British Library.

ISBN 9781787102026 (Paperback)
ISBN 9781787102033 (E-Book)
www.austinmacauley.com

First Published (2017)
Austin Macauley Publishers Ltd.
25 Canada Square
Canary Wharf
London
E14 5LQ

Dedication

Thank you to all the people who I have ever met. Thank you for your experiences, both positive and negative. You have made me, me. You have allowed me to look at life and see it for what it is – joy and pain, beauty and ugliness, love and loss. You have given me a perspective where I know normal is good, being OK is great and being good is amazing. Thank you to every single one of you. You are amazing. Dave Redman.

Contents

"The only way of finding the limits of the possible is by going beyond them into the impossible."

Arthur C. Clarke

About this Book

We all take our knocks. Life will come along and do that to you. We also get lost along the way, we forget who we are and we wonder what is the point of it all. I have taken a fair share of life's knocks. Sometimes they knocked me off course, sometimes flat on my back, and I have been so lost at times that I have wondered what is the point of it all.

But each time something bad happened I managed to find a way back, a way to stand on my feet again, to decide on what I wanted and to start moving forward, toward it, toward a brighter future.

One day I started to think about the bad things that had happened, my low points, what I had learnt and what I would do differently next time. Most importantly I thought about how I could avoid those pitfalls again. Then I started to write those thoughts down. At first they were simple mantras, my life rules, little sayings that I would refer back to and use as a buffer if life came along again and tried its worst.

These things I believed in turned into a philosophy, my philosophy for living my life, and I found that they started to help, not only when things went wrong, but also they helped when things were normal and they helped the normal to be a little better, a little brighter.

My life isn't perfect. I still get down at times and forget what I have learnt, but this book is my life philosophy about how I try to live a happy and successful life. I hope it helps you in living yours.

This book is divided into two parts, the first being the journey I went on and the second a notebook for you to fill in while you are on yours. It is structured in the same order as the chapters in this book so when you need to write something down, you can. Use it and enjoy it, because it is the key to unlocking your future, to creating your life philosophy, to being amazing.

Foreword –
Why I Needed My Philosophy

The older I got the less I understood life. Life increasingly became a constant mix of feeling anxious, worked up, frustrated, angry and that whatever I did it wasn't good enough. It seemed the harder I tried the worse things got.

I worked hard at my career and got so worked up in increasingly challenging jobs that I developed an immune system disorder. I worked myself so ragged that holidays were spent ill in bed.

I tried to please everyone other than myself and spent my time rushing around, going there, doing that, such that evenings and weekends went by in a blur. I had a constant feeling of guilt that I couldn't do enough, couldn't please everyone and that I wasn't good enough.

I read book after book from the self-help section and, although there were a few nuggets of wisdom, nothing seemed to stick. I knew something was wrong, but I just kept on ignoring the feeling, hoping it would go away, but it never did.

Then events overtook me. When I was 26 my mum suffered a brain haemorrhage (a bleed on the brain). She was critically ill and, although I didn't appreciate it at the time, what happened on the 28th of June 2003 left an indelible mark on me and for good or for bad has shaped the rest of my life.

Following the haemorrhage, Mum recovered but physically wasn't as able and had spells over the next three years where she would slip into a coma, need to be intubated (put on life support) and then would recover. To this day no one knows what caused these episodes, but each time she came back, a little more of her was left behind.

In those intervening years I did what normal people do: I continued to work hard and I met someone, which turned into a long-term relationship. But this feeling, a feeling of being out of step with the world or slightly off tune with life, didn't go away. In fact it got worse.

Then in my 29th year, with everything on the surface looking great (having just been promoted to the role of Finance Director, being engaged to be married, with the wedding booked), everything changed again. My mum passed away. She went into hospital again and never came out.

The family business, for which Mum had been the organiser, accountant and secretary, was struggling. My dad, who ran the business, had lost the only person he wanted to wake up next to in the morning and go to bed with at night.

So I thought, "This is it. I can no longer ignore this feeling of things 'not being right.' This will be my moment. This is my time to change." So that's what I did: I changed everything. Because I was unhappy in my relationship I ended it. Thinking that the family business and Dad needed me, I left my job and I went to work for him. Not being able to afford my mortgage, I rented my house and moved home.

Right now you are probably thinking that this book is all about the changes I made and how you don't need something so fundamental as the loss of a parent to do it. About how everything worked out brilliantly and that you should do the same. Well, it's not. Even after having changed things so dramatically that my present life was fundamentally different to my past, things didn't get better. They got worse.

I felt lower than ever before, less valued, more stressed and stretched. I didn't regret my decisions but I hated the reality of them. I was truly in a hole and, what was worse, it was a hole of my own making. It wasn't until one of my great friends, Scott, said something to me that I realised how low I had fallen.

After a night out I slept on Scott's sofa. I had had a fair bit to drink. It was now Saturday morning and Scotty always worked on a Saturday. He went off to work and came back that afternoon to find me in the same foetal position, nursing a hangover, trying to ignore my life. He walked in, took one look at me and said, "You won't get your boat lying there."

He was right. He knew I was in a bad place and he found a way to reach in and make me see that. It wasn't about actually having a boat; it was what the boat represented. It was a symbol of freedom and happy times, of being able to live my life how I wanted.

Up until that point, my life had been one of constant dissatisfaction with the job I had because I always thought the next one would be better. I spent years avoiding relationships for fear of being hurt instead of being brave enough to embrace the moment, even if it wasn't going to last forever. I had always tried to please other people and took no time to please myself. Then I wondered why I felt so dissatisfied with everything.

But what Scotty said really made me look at myself and think about what had happened and what I wanted. I realised the perspective from which I saw life was distorted, which meant my basis for making decisions was flawed. It was set against an expectation that I could control everything, I could know everything and that everything would go my way. I was wrong. I was very wrong.

I realised that at times, but not all the time, life is terrible and horrible and cruel. There is no reason for that. It is not about good luck or bad luck and there is no point asking 'why' when bad things happen to you, and they will happen to you. They happen to everyone.

I realised there was in fact very little I was actually in control of, I knew very little about life, and sometimes things won't go my way.

After this revelation I sunk into a deep funk and all I could think was, "What is the point!" Now I am not suggesting that I wanted to end it all, but we are talking about me thinking, "Is there anything more to life than a meaningless sequence of events and then death?"

That question never left me. It got stuck in my soul and I wanted to answer it. I wanted to know if there was more to life than death. I decided to make a conscious effort to try and understand life and what it means and then, hopefully, answer that question.

Now, ten years later, I know more truths about my life and I can honestly say I am a happier person by

14

accepting those truths. I am still learning but this is my journey and these are my truths about life. I wanted to share them with you so you can work out your truths and what life means to you (which will be different to what it means to me).

I know that you can get there. You can get there in less time than it took me, with fewer mistakes. You don't need to do what I did. More importantly, you shouldn't. You should do what you need to do and you don't need to do it all at once, rather when you are ready and in your own time. It is your life you are living, after all.

Chapter 1 –
The Test

It's Monday morning, your alarm has just gone off and you have to get up for work. How do you feel deep down inside, in your gut? Do you press snooze or do you bounce out of bed?

You have just arrived home and you are about to see someone after a day, maybe a week, or a month. How do you feel deep down inside, in your gut?

You are thinking about how you spend your time, what you do in a week or what you've done over the last twelve months. How do you feel about yourself, deep down inside, in your gut?

You are just about to leave your past behind, your job, or someone close to you. How does that feel deep down inside, in your gut?

There is a reason the phrase "gut instinct" exists. It's because it is real. Gut instinct is the clarity provided on our lives that we might not want to see.

So we ignore it, ignoring the feelings inside, closing our eyes, and we simply keep on going. But you know whether your life is rotten; you know because rotten things stink.

I left job after job because of the sinking feeling I used to get every morning. So I got a new job, and when I did, I used to say to myself that this was going to be it, this one was the job I really wanted, but after the newness of a role wore off the same old feeling would return.

Everyone I spoke to about it and probably everyone you have ever spoken to used to say something like, "Don't worry. It will get better. Just persevere for one more day/month/year and you will see, everything will be fine."

Well, you know what? It might be, but also it might not. It wasn't for me. Only you know and you do know. You know because your gut is telling you the truth. If you listen to that truth, to the feeling in your gut, you will begin to translate that feeling into a thought and that thought into pictures and then words and finally actions.

So what do you want to do about it? The easy answer is that you do nothing. You just keep on keeping on, living the same old same old. And you can. There is absolutely nothing wrong with that. You can ignore everything, fade away a little more every day until you become that bitter and angry old person you said you never wanted to be and that you promised yourself you would never become. Then you can hate yourself because now you are that person.

You could choose to go down that path or you could choose to do something different, be someone better, be that person you want to see in the morning in the mirror. You could choose to be the person you want to be. All it takes is a choice.

But, if you do choose to create a different future for yourself, you will have to do something. You will have to sort out the most important relationship in your life – t h e one you have with yourself. Here's how you start.

Chapter 2 –
Where Do I Start - Acceptance

You know that there is more to life. You just know. It is there inside of you like an ache that won't go away, or an emptiness that you try and fill up but never can. It is there when you try and please everyone other than yourself and in the exhaustion you feel at the end of every day.

You can't accept that this is how it is, because if you had you wouldn't be reading this book. I had an emptiness that I couldn't accept, that I didn't want. I wanted to feel full up, not washed out, and what made it worse was I just didn't know how the emptiness got there in the first place.

No matter how deeply I thought, I just couldn't work it out. I thought I had done everything right, working for Dad, helping out the family business, so why did I feel so bad? Then one day I stopped trying. I stopped trying to work out how I got here and why things hadn't worked out and just accepted it, that this was me right now. I was honest enough with myself to realise that things weren't great, that I had to change my life (the one I had only just dramatically changed) and that I needed to start now.

That was possibly the first time I had ever been truly honest with myself, and in accepting that truth something started to happen. There was a feeling of calmness and I began to get a sense of what could be. That was when I first started to feel positive again, and with that feeling came a deep sense of knowing that I was right to say this wasn't what I wanted. That feeling gave me the strength to ask myself, "What do I want?"

Was someone helping me? Was I being looked after and looked over? Well, some cultures believe we have a spirit guide, in others that someone is watching over us. My belief is that we carry inside of us the possibilities and opportunities to be whoever and whatever we want and that deep inside we know what that is. Life just comes along and gets in the way.

I had ignored my thoughts and feelings for so long that I had become blind to the effect my life was having on me. I had lost sight of what I wanted and more than that I didn't know who I was. Things started to change when I accepted that fact. Things started to get better when I listened to myself.

To start with I was afraid that what I was feeling was somehow wrong, that it was wrong to admit I wasn't happy, that it was wrong to say this has to change. So to help me make sense of it all I came up with and wrote down thoughts and ideas. These became my mantras, all of which are at the end of this book. The first few are:

1. Every day is a good day;
2. Don't feel bad for feeling bad; and
3. You choose.

These made sense to me because every day I was alive had to be a good day because it was a day I got to try again and try and live the life I wanted, that even though I was feeling bad I wasn't going to beat myself up about it, and that ultimately all the changes I could make came down to choice – my choice.

So please stop beating yourself up over your life; it's only you that you are hurting, after all. Accept that this is you now and be honest with what that now looks like. Then be brave enough to ask yourself the questions, "What do I want?"

Chapter 3 –
I Trust You

When was the last time someone said that to you? Well, I trust you. Over time we trust less, we doubt more and we grow tired. The reasons vary. For some it is because they have had their hearts broken; for others they have been passed over at work for that promotion or position that was promised. For some it is because a loved one has died and left them. But little by little the trust we have as children in the wonder of life disappears. The result of that erosion of trust is not just that we trust others less, but we also learn not to trust ourselves.

Once you would have thought that your mum and dad would live forever. You would have thought that if you worked hard you would get the promotion you deserved. You would have thought that your relationship with your partner would be simple and joyful. But life taught you that you were wrong, and now you think that you are always wrong, so you ignore the voice that talks to you and tells you the truth.

I did. I ignored my inner voice telling me the relationship I was in wasn't right, and knowing that, I still proposed, still started to plan a wedding, because that's what you do, isn't it? It wasn't until I spoke in honesty to a friend of mine, Alex, that I realised I had to call it off because I would be committing two people to an unhappy future.

He reminded me that I knew the truth, but I was choosing to ignore it. He said that I didn't trust myself enough because I thought I was wrong, but he told me that I should trust in what I was feeling because that is always right.

Eventually I did trust myself and ended the relationship. It was hard but it was the right thing to do, for both of us, for a happy future. I was happier without her and I know she went on to have a family (her happy ever after). You should trust yourself if you want a happy future. You should trust yourself because you are an expert in you. Here's how I know.

You have a lifetime of experiences that have made you the person you are today. If you sleep eight hours a night in one year you will gather 5,840 hours of experience. By the age of 25 you have 146,000 hours of life to draw on and reference back to. Now by my standards that makes you an expert in you and we always listen to experts and trust their opinion because they know what they are talking about.

This book is the result of a ten year journey, 58,400 hours of experience laid out for you, so that you can hopefully create the life you want in the time it takes you to read this book, rather than in the ten years it took me. It is what I trust in because it's what I know to be true.

So start trusting yourself and what you know to be true. Trust your judgment, trust the greatest expert in your life – you. You know the truth. Right now you know the truth about your life, your relationships, your work. But what has happened is that you have convinced yourself that you don't.

You keep telling yourself that tomorrow will be different, that it will be better, that things will get better, and you ignore the voice inside that is telling you the opposite, that tomorrow is going to be exactly the same as today.

So how do you reconcile the fact that the life you wanted isn't the life you are living? Does it mean your inner voice is wrong, that you are not the expert I think you are? No, it doesn't, it just means that sometimes life happens, people die and things go wrong.

But you still have a wealth of experience to draw on and from to make great decisions going forward. It means listening to your inner voice and trusting yourself, trusting your judgment. It means that things will go wrong, but it also means you will be in charge of a whole load of your life that will go very, very right.

So start believing in yourself and say to yourself, "I trust my judgment. I trust myself to know the truth when I see it, hear it or feel it."

Most importantly trust that if you have a question, if you are at a point of uncertainty and your inner self isn't talking to you, you aren't ready to make a decision. But trust that the decision, the obvious, the truth will be revealed.

My hope for you is that you start to listen to yourself again, to your inner self. It may be quiet for a while, especially if you have ignored yourself for a long time. But listen, and when you begin to hear the wisdom of your years conveyed to you in a thought, a feeling or an emotion, tune in. Then slowly but surely that sense of something will solidify into a truth for you in your life and you will start to hear the best advice anyone can give you – the advice you give yourself.

Make sure you listen and trust what you hear because you always know the truth. The only decision is whether you choose to accept it or not.

Chapter 4 –
The Relationship

Who do you love: your mum and dad; your wife or husband; your children; your dog or cat? When asked these are the typical answers everyone gives. Very few people – almost no one – say they love themselves, but the greatest and most important relationship you will ever have is with you.

It is only when your relationship with you is heading in the right direction that your life will really be heading in the right direction. If you don't love yourself, how can you love anything else? You can't. So sort out the relationship you have with yourself because from that everything else follows.

It is you who determines how good or bad this relationship is. So how do you know what this relationship is like? It comes down to a few things: how well are you treating your body; how well are you treating your mind; and how well are you treating your soul?

If you are drinking too much (you know how much is too much; you don't need me to tell you), eating loads of fast food or processed food, have no veg or fruit in your diet, not exercising at all, then your relationship with your body is bad and you will continue to feel bad.

If you aren't organised, your house or room is a mess, your work is boring, you haven't learnt anything new for ages, then your relationship with your mind is bad and you will be lost in a world of disorder and boredom.

If you are not having any new experiences, you are sitting down in front of the TV and watching the soaps all night, if you don't connect with yourself and what you want, then your relationship with your soul is bad and you will have no passion for life.

I have been in all of these three traps at one time or another, sometimes in more than one at once. When I was having a really bad time at work I drank too much. I felt lousy in the morning and work got worse. I came home and was too tired to exercise and my health deteriorated and so it went on.

The most dangerous thing about these circumstances is that we often don't realise we are there. Slowly, over time we accept more of what is bad for us and we accept that this is just how our life is.

We slowly create our own bear trap and then we don't even realise when it is sprung, when we are caught. The crazy thing about all of this is that the trap is there in front of us, but we have become so lost, so disconnected from life, that we don't even see it.

Then when we get caught and it starts to hurt we try and ignore the pain of being trapped. We attempt to block it out by doing more of what's bad for us – more food, more alcohol, more of the things that are wrong – which in the end never make your life right.

27

Now don't get me wrong. I am not suggesting that you become teetotal and a vegetarian, although that would be a very healthy lifestyle (and if you wanted to that would be great). I am saying to know what trap you are in, feel the pain and start the process of freeing yourself then healing.

How? Well, like getting out of any situation, to start with it will take an enormous amount of willpower and courage. But you owe that to yourself, don't you? You owe yourself the best life you can give you. To start with it will be painful – getting out of any trap always is – but slowly over time you will heal.

You will get stronger and you will look back and wonder how you ever allowed yourself to fall into that trap in the first place. You will wonder how you ever allowed yourself to waste so much time with a job, a life or a future that you just didn't want.

You will then have started to appreciate that the greatest relationship you can ever have is the one you have with yourself, that you need to nurture that relationship, not abuse it. Then, from that foundation, every other relationship in your life will flourish.

Chapter 5 –
The Juggernaut

Your life is like a juggernaut or an oil tanker or a runaway train. It's hard to reverse course and change direction because of the momentum you have gathered so far in the way in which you are currently living your life.

Very few people can transform their lives overnight. I am certainly not one of those, and even when I changed everything what didn't change was how I felt inside, because I changed what I was doing, not how I was feeling. We are creatures of habit and what we do over and over today will not only reinforce what we do in the future, it will reinforce how we feel in the future. And the best indication of the future is the past – that is unless you change your past.

How do you do that? It's simple: you need to change how you feel in the present. Right now, this second, I want you to grab a pen and paper and make a list of all the things that don't feel right.

You already know what is on that list. You know because you are an expert in your life. The list may not be what you want to change things to, but that's not important right now. What is important is that you write down what you want to change things from. Put it under the heading, "I owe it to me to change how I feel about the following." This is your first point of reference, like a lighthouse, shining a light on what's not right, on the rocks in your soul.

Your lighthouse (or life-house – sorry, I couldn't help myself) will allow you to see where you are in your life. Knowing that will mean you will be able to change course and avoid those dam rocks and start heading in the right direction.

And change will come, but remember you are changing course, changing direction, and the changes you want and will bring about are going to happen very gradually, slowly, almost imperceptibly, but they will happen.

They will happen because you will make them happen, and in time you will be able to look back at the journey you have undertaken and know, factually know, that you are now heading in the right direction, with the right people.

You will know because you will be able to see the journey you have been on. So write your list of things you want to change and let that list be the trigger for you to start your journey to the future you want.

Chapter 6 –

The Promise – Change Your Present

A lot of people say that they will do "that thing" some other time. It's a thing that they have been putting off for a while. They put it off yesterday, won't do it today and will find a reason for not doing it tomorrow.

Are you that person? Are you a "do it tomorrow" person? Not any more. You have already started your journey by writing your list, the most important list you are ever going to write. So what comes next? It's "The Promise".

This is the promise you are going to make to the most important person in your life. It's the promise you are making to you. But why should you do this? It is because the changes you want to make are not going to happen to you. They need to happen because of you.

If you are thinking that the ticket you bought to tonight's Euro Millions is going to solve all your problems, it won't. Your problems aren't going to be solved by money because you can't buy your way to happiness. Happiness will come about but only through change.

So promise yourself and write that promise down. Promise yourself that you are going to make one change every day. One small change. That's it. Go on, write it down after your list of the things that you are going to change.

Write down, "I promise me that I am going to change one thing every day," and sign it and date it. You have now made a contract with yourself, and what a contract! It's the most important, binding contract of your life.

Here's why it is so important. Let's imagine you have five things on your list. Let's assume that to change each one will take one hundred hours. Well, if you spent just one hour a day on it every week you could change seven percent of one item, and one hundred hours is not such a long time. It is two and a half working weeks or three full weekends or 4.167 days (you get the idea). Even if your thing took 365 hours to change (being forty-six working days) you will still have made the change within a year.

Why am I explaining this to you? Because I want to show you that you can change. So promise yourself that you will start now, do one thing every day to change your life and know that the juggernaut that is your life is turning. It is beginning to change course.

And guess what? Once you have done that one thing write it down. The date, the time, your name, and what you changed and how that made you feel. In doing this the first thing you will have changed is your present and when you look back on it tomorrow you will have changed your past as well.

I promised myself that I could get to a life I wanted to live. I promised myself that I would rebuild my life after Mum died, after I gave everything up. I didn't know what that life looked like when I made that promise; I just promised myself I would get there. Please promise yourself the same.

Chapter 7 –
Why

This is the most important word in the English dictionary. Why can create endless questions, it can reveal hidden truths and it is completely honest and without any sugar coating.

There is a reason why children use it so much. It is because they want to know. They want to understand. They want to grow and expand their minds and try and wrestle this new idea, this concept, this situation to the ground and bring it into a place where they get it.

There is a reason why adults stop using it. It is because it reveals truths to them that they find painful. It is a mirror that shows them the life they want but haven't got. It is dangerous and powerful and because of that we are afraid of it.

I questioned myself a lot about why I went to work for the family business and I realised it was for the right reasons. It was because I wanted to honour my mum's memory, I wanted to be accepted by my dad, I wanted to help the business and because it was something I had always wanted to do. But it wasn't because I had been asked to; it was because I asked to. It was then I realised the business had coped without me and would do so again, that I wasn't duty bound and if I felt it was right I could leave the business. All this came from asking myself why.

Will you start using why again? I hope so. I hope you use it a lot. Use it until people are fed up with you using it. Most importantly use it on yourself. Ask yourself, "Why am I doing this? Why does my list of things to change exist? Why have I started to change one of these things in preference to the other?" There is always a why and the answer to that question is within. You just need to be brave enough to ask it to get the answer.

Rest assured the answer is within you, but if it isn't revealed to you when you first ask yourself why, keep asking yourself. Let that computer in your head process your feelings and your experiences and reveal to you your truth. You will be able to explain to yourself why you are doing what you are doing and the more you ask the quicker and easier you will find the answers.

Why reveals the truth and when you know the truth, no matter how scared you feel, you will have the courage to change course and head in the right direction. Your fear is just you trying to keep yourself in a familiar environment, being the life you have but don't want. But a trap is still a trap, even if you are trying to convince yourself to stay in it.

Your fear is a reflection of the fact you haven't yet changed your past but you want to. Embrace the fear and love it because it is part of you. Then every time you make a change that fear will diminish a little, fade away and have less hold on you. Before you know it you won't even remember what you were afraid about in the first place. It all starts with why.

Chapter 8 –
Who You Hear

We are confronted by a multitude of voices every day: your partner; the people on the phone; the silent voices of emails and texts. They are all influencing how you think and therefore what you do.

But you know whose voice is the most important and the one that you should listen to the most and trust the most? Your own, and maybe, or probably, the relationship you have with your voice isn't a great one.

You have probably fallen into the trap of telling yourself how stupid you have been, how silly, how careless, how you have wasted your life. Well, if you are doing this over and over and over, guess what? You will begin to believe it. The trap you are in will get deeper and harder to get out of.

I was always my own worst critic, more in my personal life than my professional career. I always told myself I wasn't good enough, not handsome enough, not clever enough. It really held me back in building relationships and as soon as I began to see someone I would find a reason to end it (most of which ended up being quite ridiculous). I am not saying these people were my one true love. I just never gave myself a chance to have a proper relationship.

It was my Auntie Irene that saved me from myself because one day when I was saying some of these things she looked me in the eye and said, "Don't ever think you are not good enough, ever. You are." It was great advice and stopped the vicious cycle of self-doubt and low self-worth.

So just as my auntie said to me, I now say to you. You need to stop saying bad things about yourself because the person you hear the most is you. You need to stop saying bad things about yourself because the person whose words mean the most to you are yours. You need to stop saying bad things about yourself because the person who influences you the most is you.

So stop continually beating yourself up over the supposed mistakes you've made. Don't even think of them as mistakes, or even in terms of success or failure. Any experience that helps you move forward, toward the future you want, is a good experience, whether you feel it was a positive experience or negative experience. They are just moments in time and what is most important about these moments is that you understand what happened and why.

So be your own counsel and write down what happened and why. Most importantly write down what you learnt and what you would do differently next time. Write down how you will approach a similar problem now knowing what you know so you can create a positive outcome.

Write it down, because writing it down removes the thoughts from your brain and commits them to paper and in doing so breaks the cycle of self-flagellation that we are all guilty of sometimes.

Once you have written them down you will begin to build a reference to help you in your life, guiding you on your journey from where you are now to where you want to be. You will learn from these events and you will learn that it is not inevitable that you will make the same mistakes over and over. Quite the opposite is true: you will learn how not to make them. You will learn how to create the future you want. Then you will work out how to get there.

Chapter 9 –
Keep Learning

So you are asking yourself and others "why?" a lot. You are writing about where you feel you have something to learn from something that happened. But my guess is until you started reading this book you weren't doing those things.

So my question to you is when did it happen, that moment when you stopped? When did you stop learning? When did you think that you knew it all, or at least that you should know it all, and then, when life came along and reminded you that you know a lot less than you thought, very little in fact, what did you do?

You probably convinced yourself that what happened was a one off and that you couldn't possibly have known anything about it and that it will never happen again.

Well, maybe it was a one off and maybe it was a really bad situation that won't happen to you again. Maybe. But usually everything you experience you will keep on experiencing unless you do something to change it, unless you ask why and reflect and learn. It's when we stop asking why, when we think we know it all, that we really get in trouble. That is when we start to go backward and not forward.

So rather than being in a vicious circle repeating the same mistakes over and over, be in a virtuous circle and grow, improve and change. Find the enthusiasm again for learning, but instead of learning from a textbook or a teacher, learn from yourself about your life.

Learning is no more nor less than recording and reflecting, reflecting on what happened in the past so you can change your future. There are a whole load of experiences that you need to record, review and learn from, not least the journey that you are now on.

Your life experience is the most fantastic reference guide anyone will ever write and the best thing is it is all about you. So make sure you put pen to paper and write it down.

You don't have to write a diary, just a few lines in your notebook, and make sure you reference as many good things as bad things. Write down what happened, when, where and how, with whom and most importantly why.

We are often guilty of forgetting the good things we do, but if you create a book solely about negativity, guess what? You will be become negative, because that is the past you are leaving behind, a past which will influence your future.

It is both the good and the bad that you need to reference because both of these will help you learn and allow you to create your future, a future you want.

Chapter 10 –
Forgive Yourself

I hope you do write down your experiences. I hope that you do learn from them and change your future. You owe it to yourself to do that and you have made a promise that you will. So keep that promise because it is a promise to the most important person in your life – you.

But there is something else you need to do along with writing down your life experiences, learning from them and changing your past to create your future. You will need to forgive yourself.

For what, I don't know. But what I do know is that you will be carrying something, something inside that you or maybe someone else put there. Something that, over the time it's been in you, has grown a little, changed you a little, and these changes aren't for the better.

So you need to steady yourself because you are about to make one of the biggest changes of your life. You are going to say out loud, "I forgive myself." When I forgave myself for the mistakes I thought I had made in my life, in my relationships and in my work, I slept better, I thought less about the past and I started to look forward to my future.

So every time you feel like you are carrying that regret or guilt or hurt, you just go right ahead and say it over and over until it is all gone. You say, "I forgive myself," and when you have finished forgiving yourself, guess what? You are going to forgive all the people in your life who have hurt you, physically or mentally. You are going to say I forgive you. Not to them, because most of them won't even know that they have hurt you. You are just going to say it out loud.

Say, "I forgive you for the hurt and the pain you have caused in my life." You keep saying that until you have freed yourself of the weight of what you are carrying, of each and every hurt you have felt. Keep saying it until you have harmony in yourself because until you have harmony in yourself you cannot have harmony in your relationships.

Nelson Mandela knew this. When he was finally released after 27 years of imprisonment he called for peace, love and reconciliation because he knew that was the only way a country and a people could move forward, and he was able to do that because he forgave the people who had put him in prison in the first place. If he can do it we all can.

So the next time hurt comes your way, or the next time you blame yourself for something, simply say, "I forgive you" or "I forgive me." Because you know what? Forgiving someone is one of the best things you can do. It will always make things better.

Chapter 11 –

More of the Same Won't Make You Happy

There is a great trick that life plays on you. You are sitting there and thinking, "I am not particularly happy with my lot in life." You think, "I don't quite know what's wrong, but something is wrong."

Then you think about what it is that's wrong. But you don't think too deeply or spend too long on it; you just look at one of the main points of reference you have – your past.

So looking back at your past, and given we are talking about you before you started on your journey, you think, "What am I missing?" Here is a typical set of answers: I am missing in my life a bigger/nicer/better car; a bigger/nicer/better house; smarter/newer/fancier clothes; a flashier/smarter/quicker phone.

I know because I used to be there. I thought a bigger car, a nicer house, smarter clothes would help. I thought they would fill up all the holes in my life. All that ended up happening was I papered over the cracks and those cracks were still there, I just forgot about them for a while.

Each time I forgot I thought, "That's it, that's me sorted," but the same old emptiness came back, the same sense of longing returned and I came to realise that all of these things are short-term fixes. There is nothing wrong with a short-term fix, but what's really needed is a long-term solution.

Do you do the same? When you are feeling a bit down do you buy some new clothes or go to the pub? Don't beat yourself up. How were you to know? We only know what we have known, and if what we have known is that buying things is what we do when we are unhappy, we will do more of the same and buy more things.

But what I can guarantee you is that having more of what you currently have in your life (in the life which you want to change) is not going to give you the long-term fulfilment that you seek. You don't need more of the same. You can't buy your way to happiness. You need no more of the same and lots of something different. So what is that something different? It's whatever you want it to be. It's what the voice inside says it should be.

Chapter 12 –
What Do I Want

Where are you right now? Right at this very second? Just take a moment and look around. Whether you are lying in bed, sitting in your lounge or on a train heading home, really take in this moment because this is the moment you begin to shape your future.

You have made your list of the things you want to feel differently about. You are learning about yourself and your life and how to change your past to create your future. You are plotting your course so your life slowly evolves into what you want and you can look back and see the progress you have made. You have forgiven yourself and others, completely and unreservedly, to settle your soul. So what now?

Now is the moment of truth. This is where you cross the Rubicon[1] and move from knowing what you

---

[1] Crossing the Rubicon refers to the actions of Julius Caesar, the governor of Gaul, who crossed the Rubicon River in 49BC at the head of the 13th Legion. In so doing he crossed into Italy from Gaul where, as governor, he had authority to lead an army. This was an act of civil war and could not be undone. In modern speech "crossing the Rubicon" has come to mean committing oneself

don't want to knowing what you do want. This is where you start to move towards that destination and every day you will know you are another day closer, another 1% nearer.

But how do you know what you want? It all starts with your natural state. We all have a natural state of being, one where we are most at ease with ourselves, most alive, where everything seems to flow. To put it simply, how can you be you? Your natural state will be different to everyone else's, so you can't copy or imitate. Your natural state is not about pretending to be someone else. It's about being completely, utterly and entirely you. (How could you be anything else?)

To define this we need to list the experiences, or situations and circumstances, that connected together create a perfectly fitting whole, that provide you with your natural state.

A friend of mine, Stuart, said his natural state is where he is giving and doing the right thing. I asked him how that made him feel. He said it makes him like Stuart. I loved that. He has found the things that make him feel alive, that make him feel like he is real.

For me, I love presenting in front of people, writing, creating, spread sheets (I really do), being part of a team, being outside in the fresh air, nature, sailing, exercise, making things better. This is my natural state, and you are trying to find yours and then what it is that allows you to achieve it.

Think about your happiest times. Think about what you really enjoy doing, in the main, even if it was

---

irrevocably to a risky or dangerous course of action – the point of no return.

hard work. Think about what makes you get up in the morning with a spring in your step. Write down the situations in which you like to find yourself. Think about whom you enjoy going to see. Look back at the entries in your notebook and see if you have recorded any of these moments without realising. These are your natural states. Write these down and you will begin to sketch out a picture of who you are. Highlight those experiences or situations that make you feel alive.

That is what life is about after all, being alive, and knowing your natural state will mean you will know what your future looks like. You will know whether what you are doing today is helping you to achieve your natural state tomorrow and it will mean you will get to a tomorrow where you are living in your natural state. Then you will truly be alive.

Chapter 13 –
Stop Doing Things

Do you say yes a lot? Yes to invitations, yes to doing things during the day, yes at work, yes at home, yes, yes, yes, yes. Stop. Yes is a dangerous word and with all things dangerous it should be used sparingly.

People who say yes all the time don't know what they want for their lives and so they fill it up with other people's experiences. The yes people don't want to face the questions that lurk at the back of their mind because to do so would reveal that they don't know who they are and they don't know what they want.

If you are using yes all the time your days and nights are going to be passing by in a blur and you will finish work on a Friday and before you know it you will be faced with Monday morning and you will be thinking, "Where did my weekend go?" I will tell you: it went doing things other people wanted you to do. Which is really nice because people want you around. But the question is, is it what you wanted to do?

Some people will tell you that you should say yes to everything. I think there is a much better word. This word is no. No is empowering, no gives you freedom, no allows you to experience your life for you. No tells people you know what you want. A person who constantly says yes doesn't kNOw what they want.

But you do. You know or you are working it out. The challenge will come when, for the first time, someone asks you to come round, do something, say something, be someone and the answer that is on the tip of your tongue is no, do you say it? Well say it. Say it! Nicely, politely, but say it. Say, "No, thank you."

Nothing else is needed. You don't need to make up an excuse, don't need to say you have prior arrangements. All you need to say is, "No, thank you." Beautiful. And you will feel empowered, liberated and strong. The person may then press and ask, "Why not?" Just say, "Because it's not right for me this weekend/tonight/now."

After Mum died friends and family who had been such a great support while Mum had been unwell continued to invite us round, cooking and caring for us. They all did it because they were being kind. They did it because when Mum was ill and in the aftermath of her leaving we needed it, but slowly over time I needed it less.

When I realised that I needed it less I went round less. Some found it hard to understand but it didn't affect things long term. In fact it made things better because when we got together we really enjoyed each other's company because it was a proper catch up, and if people felt initially rejected they soon realised that I wasn't saying no forever, it was just a no, not today, thank you.

So say no a lot, say yes a little and your life will be yours and not someone else's.

Chapter 14 –

Express Yourself & Be Prepared to Be Challenged

So you have understood your why. Your why may be because you like numbers, or you like standing up in front of other people. It may be because you love to sing, or paint, or dance. It may be as simple as wanting to lose weight.

Your why could be anything, but what it is first and last is your passion. It is your soul's ambition. So now what? Well, now you start talking to people. There will be people out there who can give you some great advice. They will be people who are doing something similar to what you want to do.

It won't be exactly the same. It can't be because your life and how you want to live it will be unique (because you are unique) but it will be close and it will be a point of reference.

Find these people and ask them what changes they made to their life to get to this place, to today, to the life they wanted. Ask them what they would do differently if they had their time over. Ask them how they managed it and what were the highs and the lows. Try and understand their journey and take from them nuggets of inspiration and wisdom.

If you walk away from those discussions (and make sure you meet more than one person) feeling like you have a connection with them, that they understand you and you them, and that although you have a little fear, it has validated your decisions, stoked further the passion inside you, made your foundations a bit more concrete, then you know you are on the right course.

However, if it has made you think about whether you are making the right choices, if something just doesn't feel right, trust yourself, trust that feeling, and go back to asking yourself why. Someone said to me only recently that if something feels wrong from the start, then when you do start, it definitely will be wrong. I really like that and it helped me turn down a really good job offer because it didn't feel right.

Meeting these people will help give you inspiration and that will help to carry you along on your journey, but beware of yourself because you will try and frighten yourself away from your future.

You are trying to break the habits of a lifetime, behaviours that you no longer want, nor need, and because we are creatures of habit, fear will try and stop you. Because you are trying to create a different future for yourself, some deep misguided instinct is likely to rebel against that.

But you can tell the difference between whether your decisions are being validated or whether you need to go back to the drawing board because of how you feel in your gut.

If it feels right inside, centred, calm, excited, then you are heading in the right direction. If it feels awful inside, tight, like a stormy sea or an empty pit, then it is not right. This is because feelings, gut instinct, will tell you the truth, even if the fear is trying to convince you otherwise.

All you need to do is make sure you are taking steps that keep you headed in the right direction, and slowly and surely the fear will fade and joy will come in its place.

Chapter 15 –
Commit (Because 1% Is Important)

"There is only one thing worse than a bad decision – indecision." (I said that a long time ago.) Right now you know what you want to do. It shines bright, it is solid, and it feels good in your gut. Now commit.

Embrace your future. Love it and hold it close to you. Make it the most special relationship you have ever had. You need to pour you heart and soul into it. You need to be prepared to go the distance and that needs commitment.

You can do this. You have left behind all the things that didn't feel right. You are moving towards the future you do want and every day you will be a bit closer to your desired destination.

But remember, it is not something that will happen overnight. You need to change one percent every day and one percent a day sometimes doesn't feel like a lot. One percent doesn't give you a perspective in the moment to see how great the changes you are making actually are. One percent is nothing. That's why it's achievable. That's why one percent is important. That's why you can do it.

Commit to the one percent a day. Commit to writing down what you are doing and looking back and learning. Commit to changing your past to create your future. Commit to making a plan that brings all of these things together and commit to this for the rest of your life.

Sounds scary, doesn't it, the rest of your life? Well it shouldn't be because you know what you want. All you need to do now is make a plan about how to get there.

A plan. But what should it include? What do I put in it? How will it work?

Well, to start with your plan should be as simple as you wish and the best ones usually are.

Write down what you are going to do and when and be honest. You don't have to get it all done in the next week, but you do need to get it done in this lifetime. If you're not sure what your plan looks like talk to some more people, change a few more things and slowly you will work out what you need to do next. That is all a plan really is, a to do list, and when you have a plan nothing can stop you.

Don't leave it too long to make your decisions. Write your plan and start your journey. When you have decided, make sure you get busy on that journey. The clock is ticking and right now time is of the essence. You won't get this moment back so make it count. Don't look back, knowing what you really wanted, and think, "I should have decided sooner, started earlier." Don't leave it too late to get busy because once you start and keep going, not only will you be creating the future you want, you will be answering the voice of doubt in your mind. You will

54

be answering it by saying, "I can do this because I am doing it." So make your decisions, produce your plan and get started.

The great thing is that the more of your plan you do the more you will want to do. After you have committed and planned and acted and done that over and over the effort that it first took will disappear. You will want to take another step every day. You will want to move another one percent, change another one percent, create a bit more of the future you want, and doing so will be easy, not an effort, and more than that it will make you feel alive.

Chapter 16 –
Mount Everest (How Do I Know)

"How will I know?" This question is the most commonly asked by those people who have read this book but not started their journey. It is asked because we are afraid. We are afraid of the future. We are afraid of changing our past. We are afraid of our potential. People say, "How will I know if I have made the right choice? How will I know if I am heading in the right direction? How will I know if I have made a mistake?" You will.

Believe in yourself; that is so important. Believe. This was one of the simplest and most important mantras I wrote down. I had to believe I could make it better, better for me. To accept anything else was to accept that this was it for the rest of my life and I couldn't accept that. So I chose to believe. I chose to believe in myself.

People who climb Mount Everest believe they are going to get to the top and back down safely. Some don't. People who sail single handily around the world believe they will come home again. Some won't. Scott of the Antarctic believed he would reach the South Pole first. He didn't and he didn't come home.

But they all had a belief and they wouldn't have started their journey without it. They had belief and they prepared, they got ready and then they set off. It is no different for us here, right now. We have prepared and we have started.

The difference is we are not talking about summiting Everest or the Round the World Yacht Race. We are talking about changing your life one percent, one day at a time. So if these people believed they could succeed when faced with these challenges you need to believe in your journey and that you will complete it.

But that doesn't tell you that you have made the right decision. Belief just buys you some time before the truth has to reveal itself, and it will be revealed. How? You will know. It will happen one day, in an instant. It will be revealed the second you wake up. One day you will wake up and things will seem different. At first you won't be sure what it is and you will think, "What is different? It's not the weather, not what's for breakfast, but there is something different."

It is then you will realise that the difference is in you. That the journey you have been on has taken you far enough away from where you were to create a point of reference, allowing you to look back and realise just how far you have come.

You will know that you have now not only started your journey, but you are a good way into it. You will then know that you have reached a point of demarcation, a turning point, and from here on in you will never look back.

Chapter 17 –
Sorry

Sorry is one of the most beautiful words in the English dictionary. It is a word that carries more power, more weight and gravitas, than any other word I have ever heard or used.

Sorry disarms; it forgives and apologises. Sorry builds bridges, puts the past in the past. Sorry allows you to move forward to the future. Because whether the person you say sorry to accepts it or not, you have said it. You have done your bit. Sorry doesn't mean you're not accountable for your actions, but it does mean you have realised the implications of them.

Never be too proud to say sorry. I used to think there was only one type of sorry. I thought that sorry only existed when you had done something wrong. You had to say sorry to the person you had wronged.

Then I worked out that there are loads of different types of sorry. There is the sorry for something you have done. Then there is the sorry for when you haven't actually done anything wrong but someone feels bad. It is an "I'm sorry you feel that way" sorry.

Sorry is great. I used to use sorry a lot; now I use it more. I use it because we rarely see the world through other people's eyes. We don't get to have a third person perspective on our lives and inevitably that means we will upset people, even if we don't mean to.

So when we do saying sorry helps build a bridge, a connection between you and that other person. Sorry doesn't mean you will do something differently next time. Sorry doesn't actually mean that you have done something wrong, but sorry does mean you get the fact that what you have done or are doing is causing someone else to be uncomfortable.

Where you are going, you are going to cause some people to feel really uncomfortable. You are going to change and in changing, inevitably, you are not going to stay the same. So say sorry when people start seeing that you are not the person you were. Say sorry when people start asking why you are doing these things, moving in this direction, moving away from where you were, escaping the bear trap.

They may not get it if they are still stuck in their past and won't come with you into your future. Say sorry to these people. Say that you had to change because you just couldn't stay the same.

Chapter 18 –

Don't Let Others Bring You Down (You Are the Boss)

Where you are going you are going to be a different person to the one you were when you started reading this book and even who you are right now. How can you not be different? You are growing and learning and heading towards your destination of your choice.

You are going to encounter a lot of opinions along the way. You are going to have a lot of people tell you what they think, some because you have asked them (see Chapter 14 above), some because you have relationships with them and therefore they are in your personal rather than your professional sphere, and some because they just like to tell you what they think, especially when what you are doing doesn't agree with them.

But you need to know a really important fact about your life. In your life you don't work for anyone, you don't report to anyone, and you don't have to do anything for anyone. This is really important to remember. You get to choose. You choose whether you want to take heed of what people are saying to you. You get to choose, because you're in charge.

That's right, you heard me. You are in charge. You, no one else. You are an expert in your life. You are your own boss and you don't have to answer to anyone. NO ONE.

People will tell you why you can't do something, why you shouldn't change, why you should be grateful for what you've got. There are two things here. First, being grateful for what you have got doesn't mean that's all you should expect. You deserve the future you want; that's what you should expect.

Second, your journey reminds people that they are not on their journey. What you are doing holds up a mirror to their lives and shows them that they are not where they want to be and that they are not living, just existing. This is uncomfortable for them, uncomfortable because at some level they know this truth. They know they should be taking their journey. They know they should be making their list. They know they should be acting on their plan, but they aren't, they won't, even though they know the truth (that they should).

So instead of being brave enough to start they will try and make you stop. Because there is comfort in numbers and these individuals will try and comfort themselves by keeping you down.

So if you are faced with opposition, negativity, with people telling you why you shouldn't be on the journey you are on, remember you are the boss of your life and you get to choose. You get to choose to spend time with these people or not.

My advice is don't spend time with them because you don't need to be around people who keep you down. You know who these people are. Even now you know the people who, after you have spent time with them, make you feel a little less positive than you were before.

However, there is an important difference between challenge and negativity. You need to be challenged, but in a positive way, in a way that makes you think deeply. You should seek challenge and embrace the people that challenge you, but not the people who make you feel angry or empty or less.

So come on, grab your note pad and write down a list of names. Write down the people you want to spend less time with. Write down why. Write down the people you don't want to spend any time with. Write down why.

Your life is too short and too precious to spend another second with people you don't want to be around. After yourself the people you hear the most are the people you spend the most time with, so make sure you don't spend it with people who bring you down. Remember, you're the boss and you get to choose.

Chapter 19 –
Spend Time with People Who Lift You Up

There are so many different types of people in the world. What type of person do you surround yourself with, who are your friends, what is your family like, what type of person is your partner?

The people who you should surround yourself with should lift you up, make you feel better about life. They should give you energy, an energy to make another change, take another step, move a little faster. This may be through their challenge, their advice, their love, but they give you their energy because they care. These are the people who you should have in your life. These are the people you need to find and need to choose.

So start now. Think about the people you want to see more of and make a list of them and write down why. Now look at your previous list of the people you are going to see less of or not at all. What do you need to do? It may be a case of just switching the balance between the two groups. It may be a case of starting again. Now that you are growing and changing, you will attract different people and the people who you used to spend time with, you may not want to spend as much time with any more.

If you need to start again, think about who is missing and where you are going to find them. That's not easy. It is not easy to change the circles you mix in, change the experiences you have, but it is essential. Because the experiences you have and the experiences you have with other people create your past to reinforce your future and if your past isn't a positive one, if the people you mix with aren't pushing you forward, it is going to be harder to get there to the place where you are going.

Inevitably, when you do get there, the only people who will have come on this journey with you are going to be the positive ones, the ones who have encouraged, supported and celebrated this change. The rest you will leave behind, so make a conscious decision and leave them behind now because you will have to at some point. It's inevitable.

But if one day one of them picks up the phone, sends you a text, messages you in some way and asks for help, directly or indirectly, please help them.

They will have had their awakening and they will be asking you to share your experiences about your journey to help them on theirs, just as you had previously asked someone else to help you on yours. Help them and be part of their virtuous circle.

Help them because they will be seeking out positive people to spend time with and they have reached out to you. They want to be around your positivity so share it with them. Challenge them, help them, be part of the journey that is getting them to the future they want. Help them simply because they are asking you to.

Chapter 20 –
Value the Good You Have in Your Life

There are some things that are really right with your life. If not some things then definitely one thing because no one has a life where everything is wrong, and I can guarantee you that the one thing that is right with your life is the fact that you are alive.

It is important to know this because there is a temptation to change everything, start again, like you have deleted your past (which is what I did without great results). You don't need to change everything. You don't need to get rid of all of the relationships you have in your life. You just need to change what needs to change.

You may want to change a lot, reshape your life loads, but for those things, people, loved ones in your life who already have real meaning, you don't need to change a thing about them and you don't need to change how you are with them.

Instead you need to recognise who and what these relationships are and you need to make sure you value them, that you embrace and love them, and don't lose sight of them.

So go on your journey, embrace your future, but in all of that you shouldn't leave everything behind. Love what you have that is worthy of your love and make sure that you keep on giving your love.

These are the people who have got you here, and these are the people who will help get you to tomorrow and give you the love and support when tomorrow seems a long way away.

These will be your shelter from stormy seas, your sun on a cloudy day, your love of life when you feel empty. You already have good in your life without changing anything, so make sure if you change almost everything you don't change and lose the love you already have and enjoy.

Instead value, invest in and enjoy it. It's there because of who you are and because of the love that people already want to give to you. Let them give that love to you and cherish it when they do, giving all the love you have back to them.

Chapter 21 –
Enjoy the Journey

What is the point of the journey? It is to get where you want to go, to the destination you wish to arrive at. But there is something very important that you need to know that will make the journey all the more sweet and the destination worthwhile.

This is that the pleasure of the destination is to be found in the journey itself. Does that make sense? Let me explain. You are trying, you are changing, you are growing, and you are spending time with people who you wish to spend time with.

But what is the point of that if you can't enjoy the moment? The destination is only fifty percent of the reason for doing what you are doing. The other fifty percent is actually doing it.

It is not until we learn to appreciate the moment that we can truly reach our destination. The moment is all we have right now, right at this second. You are going to change what that moment looks like but at this very moment this is your moment.

So look around you and take in what you are seeing, what you are doing, what others are doing. Take in where you are and breathe. Breathe all of it in like a breath of fresh air because this moment is never going to be repeated.

So enjoy the people around you, appreciate the fact that they are sharing in your journey by being in this moment with you. Embrace the struggle if that is what you are currently facing. But savour the moment like it is the tastiest thing you have ever eaten.

Every second of every day is a gift. You have just got to be open to receiving that gift and using it to help you create the future you wish. Someone said to me the other day that they wished it were Christmas again. Well, from now on every day for you can be Christmas day, or your birthday, or Easter (whichever day is your favourite day) because every day you will be given a gift, so enjoy it. Enjoy the gift that is now.

Chapter 22 –
Give/Sell/Throw Away Your Past

How much stuff have you got? People often talk about emotional baggage, but our whole physical world defines us: our clothes, our furniture, our homes, our cars, our lives. Mentally, emotionally, physically, you can't possibly take all of this with you into your future.

All of this is the person you were. It ties you to your past. It weighs you down and makes it harder for you to get to the future you want. In forgiving people and yourself you have dealt with your emotional load. You know you are lighter now on the inside, sleeping a little better, feeling a little brighter, thinking a little clearer. Now you need to deal with your physical load. Now you need to deal with what's on the outside.

So look around you right now. What is dusty and messy and cluttered? What haven't you worn for years, what has never come out of the cupboard, what don't you like the look of any more? Things only have the meaning we attach to them. If you tell yourself you can't get rid of something, guess what? You can't.

I kept old CDs I hadn't listened to in years, books I would never read again, bank statements for the last three years. Why? Because I couldn't let go of my past. Then one day I got a load of heavy-duty bin bags and just cleared the lot, giving anything that was good to charity.

It was actually a pretty traumatic experience but the next day I knew I had moved a little further forward and that I would move a little quicker in the future because I wasn't weighed down by all the things from my past.

If you realise these things are a reflection of the old you, the you of a long time ago, and this is not you now, these things won't mean the same. They may in fact mean very little and it is these things you need to get rid of. One at a time, one thing, every day until your load has lightened.

That's all, just one thing every day, and before you know it within a month you will have cleared thirty (or twenty-eight or thirty-one, depending on the month) items of clutter from your life. Thirty less things to sift through, dust, move, but generally never use. What a waste of your time keeping all these things has been.

But, the things that are still precious to you, the keepsakes, the photos, the trinkets, the things that feel warm when you pick them up because the feeling is on the inside, these are the things that you should keep.

These are the things that reflect the beauty in your life and should not be put aside, given away or sold, the little things which mark the passage of time and your passing through life. We should always leave a clue about where we have come from, just in case we get lost along the way and have to retrace our steps.

Chapter 23 –
Writing Is Remembering

One of the most important disciplines you will need to help you in your journey is taking just a moment to write things down: your lists, your feelings, your future.

Unless you have a photographic memory and you can remember everything that happens in your life, you will forget, and if you forget you run the risk of repeating the mistakes of your past.

The notes you make will not only provide guidance for the journey you are on right now, but they will also be a point of reference for the rest of your life.

They will be there for when you have got a tough decision to make or you are faced with a difficult situation, so don't forget them because they will always be there to look back on.

You will be able to look back on yourself, seeing what you did last time, how you felt and the outcome of the situation.

You will be able to see patterns emerging, ones to either change or to reinforce. You will create a guidebook to your life and the guide, holding that book and using it, will be you.

But without these notes, without this book, for which you are the author, the ability to translate your past into your future will be lost. The journey you will have taken will be forgotten and the learning you went through only vaguely remembered.

So please record your journey because it will not only help you now, but it will become an invaluable guide for the rest of your life. I am still creating my guidebook because you never stop learning, and time and again it has proved invaluable in helping me make good decisions (or at least let me learn from bad ones).

Chapter 25 –

Be Ready for the Good Things When They Happen

I can promise you, guarantee you in fact, that when you start making the changes you want to make, when you start to move towards the future you want to create, life will come along and help you out.

It will provide opportunities for you to be able to move a little faster, maybe get there a little quicker, and you will be thinking, "Wow, that was lucky" or "I can't believe it, something is going my way for a change."

But it's not luck, it is not chance, it is not a random event that has given you this boost, this opportunity, in this moment: it is you. You have created it with the positive momentum you have built for your life, the life that is now heading in the right direction.

The old you, in your old life, would not have been able to take advantage of this "good luck". But it's not random luck; it's your luck. A great friend of mine, Dom, once said, "You create your own luck," and that is what you are now doing. You are creating your own luck.

So be ready for that. Be ready to accept that good things can and do happen to people and they will happen to you. Be ready to open your arms wide and embrace (metaphorically or physically) the opportunities that come your way.

I say this because it is easy to slip into a rut where you begin to get scared of the future. You start to think you don't deserve these good things, that they don't and shouldn't happen to you, so you don't take life up on its offer. Instead you decline and begin again the decline back to where you came from.

Please don't do that. Don't doubt yourself; trust yourself. Don't say you don't deserve it; know you do deserve it. Know that the changes you are making in your life are creating your own luck and don't be afraid of that. Be brave and allow yourself to enjoy life when it comes along and helps you out because it will.

Chapter 25 –
Create Your Own Reality

Do you know what one of the scariest things is about life? Not work, not holidays – no, life. We really don't know what is in store for us and I know we like to know. We like certainty. Of course we do. We are all creatures of habit and so what we tend to do is repeat the same experiences, see the same people and do the same things over and over because it is what we know, because it makes us feel secure.

Well, that is fine if these experiences are keeping you on course, if they mean you are getting a little closer to your destination every day. My guess is though that they aren't. All they are doing is keeping you in the same reality you have always been in, holding you back.

So here is one of the most important things you will ever hear in your life. You are not a victim of circumstance. You are not a passenger in your life. You know you are your own boss, no one else, and with this knowledge you need to know that you create your own reality.

What you do, what you say, who you see, the decisions you make, the steps you take all begin to create the reality that is your future. Your actions will begin to leave behind a past that is closer to the tomorrow you want, closer than it was yesterday and the day before that and the day before that.

You create your own reality. So create it. Write it down. Grab your notebook and write down what your perfect week looks like. Write down whom you would see, what you would do, how you would do it and what the result of all of this would be. Imagine the future you want in terms of your morning, your afternoon and your evening. Imagine it in terms of your days and your nights. Imagine it in terms of your whole life.

So many people don't achieve the life they want simply because they aren't brave enough to imagine that it could happen. Well, unless you write it down it will never happen. So imagine, really imagine what your future looks. Imagine your perfect week and write that down.

Now look at your lists, the first being what you want to change, the second being what you want and the third being what those changes look like in terms of how you will spend your days and weeks. Then look at your plan. This is how you will get there. All of this is your reality; all you need to do now is create it.

Chapter 26 –

Know What You Can Control and then Surrender to the Universe

We go through life thinking we can control everything. We plan and sweat and toil to try and ensure we know what's happening next, what tomorrow brings, what our future holds. But then things don't go our way. Life happens and we get really upset. When things don't go our way, that's life reminding us of the one truth: we are not in control.

We are not in control of our loved one's health. We are not in control of whether we get a promotion. We are not in control of other drivers on the road, the rain, the sun, the traffic. All we can do is influence them. All we can do is play the odds.

The better we eat, the more we exercise, the greater our chances of living a healthy life. The harder we work (not longer, harder), the more we learn, the greater our chances of getting that promotion. The better we drive, the more we follow the highway code, the more aware other drivers will be of our intentions and the less chance there will be of an accident.

But accidents do happen, on the road, in life. Loved ones die, relationships end, things sometimes just don't work out. This book, your journey, does not guarantee you will beat these odds. You won't live forever, you won't avoid illness or old age, but what you will do is have the ride of your life.

You will be heading in the right direction, even if life derails you. But because you know what you want and because you are headed in the right direction, because you are surrounded by people who love you and who support you, because you have changed one percent every day, you are more prepared, more able to deal with it.

So don't rely on luck (and there are some lucky people out there). Don't rely on someone else (and some people do, a lot). Make sure you rely on you and remember life is alive and you cannot control that. What you can control is what happens in the moments of calm between the storms. What you can control is how you spend your time, when you have that time for you. So spend it well, with people you want to be around, in a world you have created, in your reality, and it will be amazing.

Chapter 27 –
Final Thoughts

Are you different? I think so. I think you are a dreamer and a doer. People would say those two don't go hand in hand, but unless you have a dream, how can you do anything to achieve it?

You always had a sense that things weren't quite right with your life, and as you got older that feeling didn't go away. It didn't go away even if you changed jobs, changed houses and sometimes even changed relationships.

But life has a way of being kind and it was kind enough to put us together. Slowly and surely we realised that there was more than one person who thought the way we did. There were two people: you and I.

Now we hope there are more than two. Maybe there is just one more. We know that right now having read this book the journey has started and that the journey is going to be amazing.

We hope that in starting our journey we will inspire people to start their journey, and four dreamers and doers will become eight, sixteen, and then thirty-two and so on and so forth until everyone in the UK is heading in the direction they want, doing what they want and being who they really are, and do you know how long this would take?

If everyone who read this book suggested to only one person that they read this book and this happens every month, after three years this message would have reached every person in the UK.

This is what we imagined when we imagined our future, a future where we know the truth. One where we understand what we do want and what we don't want. A future we are creating for ourselves and where we are not alone on our journey.

Rest assured you are not alone on your journey because right now there are others reaching for the future, just as you are, so please help them. Share some of what you are going through to help them with what they are going through. Just send us an email using the address below and we will share your journey with others to help them on theirs.

thisismyjourney@thinkamazingbeamazing.co.uk

Chapter 28 –
My Journey

Finally, to share some of my journey, here are all of my life philosophies that led to this book:

1. Everyday is a good day;
2. Don't feel bad for feeling bad;
3. You choose;
4. Don't let others bring you down;
5. Believe;
6. Anything is possible;
7. Think amazing to be amazing;
8. The only limitations we suffer are those imposed by ourselves;
9. Know when you've made a mistake;
10. Never be too proud to be sorry;
11. To get the right answer be clear on the question;
12. Give someone a gift everyday;
13. You always learn;
14. Don't be bullied;
15. Say thank you;
16. Invest in people, relationships, friendships;
17. Listen;
18. Lead by example;
19. Don't control;

20. Be valued; and

21. Care.

Good luck, but you won't need it. Why? Because you have already got everything you need to get there, to the future you want.

You have got you.

Epilogue – January 2016

You may need this book more than once. If you do a new notebook can be requested from the website: www.thinkamazingbeamazing.co.uk

You may need to create your own reality several times over. It is unlikely your journey is finite. Probably it will be a journey where you will need to start from the place where you feel you have just finished.

That is because life is alive and we can't control that. Two weeks after finishing this book life came along and reminded me that I am not in control. All we have is the moment and the journey.

The last few years for me have been difficult. The year before our wedding my wife's mother was diagnosed with lung cancer. Arranging a wedding, dealing with a terminal illness and trying to keep your life on track, along with the lives of the people that you love, is tough.

Three months after we were married my mother-in-law passed away peacefully at home on Christmas Eve. I was there when it happened and there to support my wife and her dad and sister over the twelve months that followed.

Never underestimate what the loss of a parent will do to a relationship and to a person. We had a tough year, but I knew what that looked like. I had been there before. We had a tough year, but I loved her and I believed in our future.

Then a week ago my wife came home and said that she wasn't in love with me. That she couldn't give me what I deserved. That she was leaving me. I was, am, heartbroken.

My life isn't perfect. I still get down at times and forget what I have learnt, but this book is my life philosophy about how I try to live a happy and successful life. I hope it helps you in living yours. It is just about to start helping me again in living mine.

Dave

Your Think Amazing Be Amazing Notebook

This Notebook

This notebook accompanies the main book and references the parts where you make a pledge or a commitment.

It is structured so you can write down your lists and record your thoughts in the same order as the book is written.

This is your guide to create the life you want so please make it a good one.

The Trust Yourself Statement

You need to start trusting yourself again. Trust your judgment, trust the wisdom of your years, trust your feelings.

From chapter 3 copy out the pledge to trust yourself again, or write your own, and then sign and date it.

....
....
....
....
....
....

Signed...

Dated...

Things That Don't Feel Right in My Life

What is it that doesn't feel right in your life? What do you want to change? Write those things down. You don't need to know what your future looks like right now. You just need to know what you want to change. Think about your list and write it down. You owe it to yourself to change how you feel about the following:

………..……………………………………………..
……………………………………………………………
…………………………………………………………….
………………………………………………………….…
…………………………………………………………….
…………………………………………………………….
…………………………………………………………….
…………………………………………………………….
…………………………………………………………….
…………………………………………………………….
…………………………………………………………….
…………………………………………………………….
…………………………………………………………….
…………………………………………………………….
…………………………………………………………….
…………………………………………………………….
…………………………………………………………….
…………………………………………………………….

....
....
....
....
....
....
....
....
....
....
....
....
....
....
....
....
....
....
....
....
....
....
....
....
....
....
....
....
....
....
....

The Promise to Change

Make a promise to the most important person in your life: you. From chapter 6 copy out the promise, or write your own, and sign and date it. The promise is:

…………………………………………………………….
…………………………………………………………….
……………………………………………………………...

Signed……………………………………………

Dated……………………………………………

What I Changed Today and Tomorrow and the Day After...

Now that you are changing one thing every day you need to write that down, what you did, when and how that made you feel. This is so you can look back and see your life is changing and that you are making that happen. Don't forget to sign and date each entry you make. You wouldn't want someone else taking the credit.

....
....
....
....
....
....
....
....
....
....
....
....
....
....

....
....
....
....
....
....
....
....
....
....
....
....
....
....
....
....
....
....
....
....
....
....
....
....
....
....
....
....
....
....
....
....
....
....
....

I Would Do This Differently Next Time

Don't beat yourself up about what you think you did wrong, but do learn from it. So write it down, whatever it is and what you did. Write down how the situation arose, what you learnt and what you would do differently next time.

....
....
....
....
....
....
....
....
....
....
....
....
....
....
....
....

I Did a Good Thing

So write it down. You need to record all the good things, the things you got right, that you did today. Be the author of your guide through life and give yourself the best education you can, one based on you.

....
....
....
....
....
....
....
....
....
....
....
....
....
....
....
....
....
....
....
....
....

I Forgive Myself

....
(Your name here)

I forgive all the people that have caused hurt and pain in my life

....
(Your name here)

My Natural State

List the things you like to do. Write down the situations in which you like to find yourself. Make note of the challenges you love, what you love doing and when you love doing them. Then understand why you love them because in so doing you will understand you. You will begin to create a picture of your natural state.

....

....

....

....

....

....

....

....

....

....

....

....

....

....

....

....

....
....
....
....
....
....
....
....
....
....
....
....
....
....
....
....
....
....
....
....
....
....
....
....
....
....
....
....
....
....
....
....
....
....

What I Took From Meeting You

Find the people you want to speak to and work out what you want to ask them. Every time you meet one of them you will think differently about the next person, so if there is a preference to who you would like to see, put the favourite person last, because by then you will know a whole lot more than you do now and you will have a clearer idea of what you want to ask. So go on, make your list, write your questions and leave plenty of room for notes for when you do meet that person.

These are the people I want to see, this is what I want to ask and this is what I learnt when I met you:

....
....
....
....
....
....
....
....
....
....

....
....
....
....
....
....
....
....
....
....
....
....
....
....
....
....
....
....
....
....
....
....
....
....
....
....
....
....
....
....
....
....
....
....
....

My Plan

These are the things I am going to do and this is by when. This plan will help get me from today to the tomorrow I want, so I am going to make sure I am honest with what I can achieve and I am going to make sure I achieve it because I only have one lifetime to get this right. This is my life to do list:

....
....
....
....
....
....
....
....
....
....
....
....
....
....
....
....
....

....
....
....
....
....
....
....
....
....
....
....
....
....
....
....
....
....
....
....
....
....
....
....
....
....
....
....
....
....
....
....
....
....

....
....
....
....
....
....
....
....
....
....
....
....
....
....
....
....
....
....
....
....
....
....
....
....
....
....
....
....
....
....
....
....
....

These Are the People I Am Going to Spend Less Time with and This Is Why

....
....
....
....
....
....
....
....
....
....
....
....
....
....
....
....
....
....
....
....
....
....
....
....

....
....
....
....
....
....
....
....
....
....
....
....
....
....
....
....
....
....
....
....
....
....
....
....
....
....
....
....
....
....
....
....
....

These Are the People I Am Going to Spend No Time with and This Is Why

....
....
....
....
....
....
....
....
....
....
....
....
....
....
....
....
....
....
....
....
....
....

These Are the People I Am Going to Spend More Time with and This Is Why

....
....
....
....
....
....
....
....
....
....
....
....
....
....
....
....
....
....
....
....
....
....
....

These Are the People and the Things That I Love

In everything that you are going to change, these are the people and things that you value and that you will make sure will remain the same.

....
....
....
....
....
....
....
....
....
....
....
....
....
....
....
....
....
....
....
....

My Perfect Week Looks Like This

....
....
....
....
....
....
....
....
....
....
....
....
....
....
....
....
....
....
....
....
....
....
....
....

This is Me living

....
(your name here)